Copyright © 2025 by
Dr. Maunda Charles

All rights reserved. This book or any portion thereof may not be reproduced or used in any manner whatsoever without the express written permission of the publisher except for the use of brief quotations in a book review.

Printed in the
United States of America
First Printing, 2019

2nd Edition, v2
ISBN: 979-8-218-61481-2

Published by PurposefulTime, LLC
www.purposefultime.com

*This book is dedicated to my parents,
Drs. Vincent and Fenella Cooper*

Foreword

It is an absolute honor for me to write this foreword for Dr. Maunda Charles about a topic that is so important to the body of Christ, as well as the world. I met Dr. Charles as a partner of our ministry and became more familiar with her excellent ability to manage being a wife, mother, minister, and a career with such grace.

The wisdom and tools that Dr. Charles gives in this book will enable you to maximize the seasons that you are in, with the help of the Holy Spirit, while focusing on what God has called you to, instead of living life in frustration, trying to juggle a myriad of purposeless activities and assignments.

I thank God for Dr. Charles and her heart to serve people in wanting to see them leading purposeful, stress-free lives through properly managing our lives.

Dr. DeeDee Freeman
Faith City Central
(formerly Spirit of Faith Christian Center)

Acknowledgments

Thanks be to God for the great things he has done in me, for me and through me! For many years I have been told that I should write a book on time management. As I pondered, wondering when and how, this thought stayed at the back of my mind until I really focused on my purpose.

I am thankful for my family and friends that have convinced me of the need for this book. I am especially grateful for my husband, and his unwavering support for me to have the desires of my heart. He allows me the flexibility (without any pressure), to dedicate my time to fulfilling purpose, while serving as the Chief Family Officer of our home, after working outside of the home for the first 15 years of our marriage. Of course, I am thankful for our five children, my first clients. It is because of them that my focus on purposeful time management became a requirement for my sanity!

Special appreciation goes to my pastors, Apostle Michael A. Freeman and Dr. DeeDee Freeman, for the awesome teaching examples that they are to my family and the body of Christ at large. They continue to challenge me to fulfill the purpose and calling for which I have been prepared, for such a time as this!

*To every thing there is a season, and a **TIME** to every **PURPOSE** under the heaven:*

Ecclesiastes 3:1 KJV
(Emphasis added)

There are three things in life that we must master -
1. *Change*
2. **Time**
3. *Self-awareness*

Apostle Michael A. Freeman
Faith City Central

TABLE OF CONTENTS

Time to Testify!... 1

Introduction – Master Your Time............... 5

1 o'clock: Wait A Minute!........................... 11

2 o'clock: Time Management or Priority Management.. 19

3 o'clock: 'Work-Life Balance', a Misnomer.. 25

4 o'clock: Goal Setting, Getting, and Timing... 39

5 o'clock: Time Management Essentials..... 49

    5:15 - RECAP.................................. 63

    5:30 - Dr. Charles' Quotes for Time Management Success....................... 65

6 o'clock: My Time (About Dr. Charles)... 67

7 o'clock: Family Time........................... 73

8 o'clock: Discovering your Purpose......... 89

Time to Testify!

PurposefulTime is not just a business that teaches you how to be on time for work or how to make every minute count. It is a program that encourages you to use your time in a way that adds value and meaning to your day. When I began consulting with PurposefulTime, I was pretty established in managing my time because time management played a big part in my profession. However, I decided to invest in PurposefulTime so that I could reassess how I spent my time after having a second child and dealing with life experiences. I knew how to manage my time, but everything just seemed so fast-paced and with no self-fulfillment.

When I spoke with Dr. Maunda, one of the things that I remember her telling me was, when it comes to your family and your day-to-day tasks, it should be enjoyable. When you spend time with your family, it shouldn't feel like you have just checked another item off of your list of to do's. You should be having
fun with your family. Well, when you have what was then a 2 and a 6yr old, it can feel like everyone is having fun but you. Learning to find enjoyment while managing my time has helped me to see time management from a different perspective. Two years later I can say that I have found enjoyment in doing my daily tasks and I am enjoying my family more and more each day.

Thank you PurposefulTime for helping to bring value and meaning to my day-to-day tasks.

M. Brown

As a graduate student that works part-time and serves in ministry full-time, I felt overwhelmed. I thought that this season in my life was going to be about finding a perfect balance. PurposefulTime helped me to see that managing time is not only about finding balance, but about prioritizing my responsibilities.

I initially struggled to comply with the schedule because I had never experienced so much structure in my schedule. Once I allowed PurposeTime to become the pastor over my time and the Holy Spirit to guide me when things did not go as planned, my perspective on time management changed. I am still a work in progress, but Dr. Maunda has always been a helpful and firm accountability partner. I am truly grateful for PurposefulTime. Now that I understand the importance of prioritizing time, I feel more at peace, even in the midst of my busy schedule.

R. H.

I know that I've had a problem with time management for some time now. My boss has mentioned it. My mentor has mentioned it. My family and teammates usually just roll their eyes if I'm late or behind on something. So, I knew it was a problem. I knew I needed to do something about it, but didn't know what. That's when I stumbled upon a social media post from PurposefulTime. It was talking about how multitasking is really not multitasking at all, but starting and stopping, and not finishing the first thing you were doing. That stuck with me.

I knew Dr. Maunda was the person that could help. I went from multitasking, starting and not finishing, to focusing and prioritizing my activities. I went from not knowing where my time went to scheduling my time, including cooking, shopping, reading, writing, and spending time with my kids. Instead of feeling frustrated, I now feel peace. I say "no" more to time wasters and am more intentional with the one thing I can't get back, my time. Thank you, Dr. Maunda!

Y. Bright

My daily routine was filled with many activities that all sat on my mind constantly, as I tried to figure out how to organize my life. It was very burdensome as I contemplated what needed to be done and what could wait. In my mind's reality, everything needed to be done, but nothing actually got done.

When Dr. Maunda Charles shared her services of time management with me, it was a breath of fresh air. She helped me organize my days into realistic, actionable routines that I could easily follow. My previously burdened mind became free and open to think on my planned activities and execute them. I am grateful to Dr. Maunda for all the time she poured into making me a better person and I'd highly recommend her services to anyone looking to transform and organize their daily routine.

K. Credle

Introduction
Master Your Time

Master your time.

Don't let time master you!

So much to do, so 'little' time...

We've all said this at some point. However, once we realize that WE are the MASTERS of our time, our time will no longer master us! Over the next couple of days, I will share with you some Time Management Essentials (TMEs) to help you perfect your time management skills. If you follow the TMEs and carry out the tasks right away, you will create your own time management plan by the end of this book.

However, if you don't have the time (pun intended), I can help you. (Actually, everyone has the time. It's how we choose to prioritize it that determines what we do with it.) For more information visit my website.

www.purposefultime.com

Procrastination, the enemy to success

Procrastination not only delays your tasks, it potentially delays your purpose!

It was very important to me that we start off this journey by identifying those habits that are hindering you from reaching your goals. Procrastination is one of the biggest hinderances to time management success.

By definition procrastination means:

1. to put off intentionally and habitually

2. to put off intentionally the doing of something that should be done

Why do people procrastinate?

Unfortunately, many of us procrastinate because we are overwhelmed, lazy, lack confidence, fear failure or hope that task will eventually go away, or someone else will do it (*www.lifescript.com*). The fact of the matter is if you want someone else to control your destiny, then you should continue to procrastinate.

However, overcoming procrastination requires that YOU become accountable for your success. Ineffective time managers procrastinate because they don't have a grasp on the importance and value of their time. Putting things off for another day gives them a sense of temporary freedom today when, in actuality, it is setting up a cycle of scheduling conflicts, and delays tomorrow. In order to take control of your time, procrastination must not be a practice. ***Don't give up the permanent fulfillment of purpose for the temporary satisfaction of some 'free time'. You will pay for it in the end!***

I am very excited about this journey that we have both committed to and guarantee that you will become a BOSS at time management if you stay the course. Feel free to share this with your family and friends. Encourage them to take this journey with you and become your accountability partner(s). Success is always better when you can achieve it with someone else. Let's redeem the time together, one minute at a time!

"Everyone has the time, it's how we choose to prioritize it that determines what we do with it."

Chapter Notes

1

Wait a Minute

Wait A Minute!

As we think about everything that we have on our plates, we are often tired before we even get started. Then the kids, your spouse, your boss, a friend or someone else wants to add one more serving to your already overloaded plate. 'Wait, I just need a minute!" you exclaim.

If you can visualize a plate of food, think about how some people don't like their food to touch, others couldn't care less, and there are others that like to mix everything together. Now, see your plate as a clock. Your protein may take up one-fourth of the plate, say 12 o'clock to 3 o'clock. Then your starch may take up another quarter, from 3 o'clock to 6 o'clock. And finally, your veggies may take up the other half of the plate, from 6 o'clock to 12 o'clock (Well maybe that's just my plate. I like veggies...LOL)

The way that we divide or schedule our time may be similar to the visualization of food on our plates. Some people designate times for everything that they do and don't allow their activities to overlap, or food to touch. Others keep a 'healthy' separation between their activities but don't mind if there is some comingling of sauces now and again. However, there are others who do thrive off of intentionally mixing everything together, except sometimes you really can't tell what they are eating (accomplishing).

"Your commitment... will be the difference in whether you become the manager or the managed."

Just like there is only so much food that you can pile on a plate, there is also a limit on the amount of time we have. An overloaded plate will get heavy and eventually topple over onto the floor (hit rock bottom). Maintaining an overloaded schedule will inevitably spill over into other areas of your life, including your health (physical, mental and emotional), your finances and your relationships. Although no one wants to find themselves in any of these extreme situations, we can all end up there if we don't take introspect. This is when we really need to pause and say, 'Wait a Minute!"

Honesty is the Best Policy

Be honest with yourself about where you are. If you don't acknowledge it internally, you will continue to go in circles, because real change comes from locating yourself within. Once you have located yourself, you can create a roadmap from your current situation to your desired destination.

This journey to becoming a better time manager involves several steps. Your commitment to changing the way that you think about and manage your time will be the difference in whether you become the manager or 'the managed'.

Contrary to popular belief, knowledge is not power. APPLIED knowledge is power! Throughout this book, you will be given assignments so that you can apply what you are learning. Please do the assignments within one to two weeks to ensure that you stay on track. You will learn a lot during this time, but it is the application of this information that will help you to retain and repeat what you've learned. There is a saying that 'knowledge is power', but that is inaccurate. If that were the case a bookshelf, or better yet, your local library would be very powerful for just having information. Knowledge is available all around us. But, **applied** knowledge is power.

Do not move forward to the next session without completing the prior assignment(s) as they are building blocks for the next steps. There is a reason that our educational system is organized in levels. You don't go from first grade straight to 10th grade. There is some incremental learning that must take place. There is some application to be done and some tests to pass or prove that you understand what you have learned. Such is the case with this book. Don't be in such a hurry to complete it that you miss out on the essential nuggets throughout. Complete all of the assignments with the greatest level of effort possible. What you get out of it is a direct result of what you put into it. Application of these principles will make how you spend your time more purposeful.

Are you intentional about how you spend your time? Isn't it interesting how we say that we are spending time doing X, Y, and Z? Time is costly. We can either spend it, waste it or invest it. You can tell which one you have done by the corresponding return that you receive.

Ultimately, how we use our time should directly correlate to our purpose in life. From time to time we should pause to reflect on how we are really allocating our time. Your time is not only precious, it is prophetic. So, use it purposefully!

Surveys show that social media, television, and phone calls are some of the greatest time thieves. I would also add oversleeping and laziness to that list. The clock is ticking. Do you want to drift through life aimlessly, or do you want to accomplish what you have been put on this earth to do, with the time that you have? Unfortunately, when we don't maximize our time, our purpose is diverted, delayed, or even denied. So, let's make meaningful movements, remain focused and arrest the time thieves. 'Wait a Minute'! It's time to fulfill purpose!

Chapter Notes

2

Time Management

Or

Priority Management?

Time Management

Or

Priority Management

What's the Difference?

We always have time for what we prioritize.

As we hustle and bustle through our week, we are often challenged with 'not having enough time'. But, why don't we? Is that really true? We all have 24 hours in a day, but yet it seems like there's always something left undone. Why don't we have the time to do the things that we want to do? Well, have you considered that you might be doing things that you don't need to do?

Or, maybe you aren't doing the things that you should be doing? The truth is, if I take a quick look at your schedule, I can tell what is important to you. Remember, we always have time for what we prioritize!

So, what does that mean? Well, our time can be stretched into several different directions. I mean, we have to work, spend time with our families, take the kids to their activities, serve in church or volunteer organizations, go to the gym, have some girl time/man time, etc. Oh, and we must have time for ourselves, right? Well, the truth of the matter is that we are way TOO busy. And whose fault is that? Yep, yours. (sigh) But, you can change that! (smile)

The fact is, WE CONTROL OUR OWN SCHEDULES!

Some of you might disagree, but think about this... All of the extra-curricular activities that we commit to are just that....EXTRA, which means we don't HAVE TO do them! Yes, we have to work, but do we have to work THAT schedule? Yes, we want to have well-rounded kids, but do they have to be involved in EVERY activity, especially if it has nothing to do with their gifts or calling in life? If we are truly living in the will of God for our lives, then why is our schedule out of whack? We are doing everything He wants us to do, right...maybe not. God has graced us to do everything that we are supposed to do. Key phrase, SUPPOSED TO DO. There is no grace for things that you should not be doing. So, with this understanding, how can we control our schedules better? How can we manage our time according to His will? Ecclesiastes 3:1 says, *"To every thing there is a season, and a time to every purpose under the heaven"*. So, there is a purpose for every minute of your day and there is a time for every purpose! You just need to know what you should be doing and when you should be doing it. The key here is prioritizing your life.

"Focus on those things that attract and attach you to your purpose, not those that detract or distract you from your purpose."

What takes precedence? Many of us say that we are putting God first, but are we really? Does He come before our jobs, our spouses, our kids, our hobbies, etc.? How much quality time are we investing in the things that we say matter to us?

We need to identify the 'time thieves'! I've been guilty of not prioritizing God or the time that He has given to me. (Did you say 'ME TOO'?) Well, maybe it's time to take introspect. When is the last time you reviewed your weekly or monthly schedule to determine if you are really prioritizing the things or the people that you say you value? The only way to track progress is to measure it.

Because change is inevitable, we must constantly evaluate where we are on our way to where we are going. We all want better, but better doesn't just happen.

Improvement in any area requires a greater investment of our time. We see the truth of that statement in the lives of any successful businessperson, athlete, student, etc. Focus on those things that attract and attach you to your purpose, not those that detract or distract you from your purpose. So, make a commitment to yourself today to make your time purposeful! Now, who has the time? You do!

PurposefulTime tips to maximize your minutes:

1. Make a list of your priorities
2. If you don't currently have one, create a draft of your current weekly schedule
3. Compare your priorities to your schedule and determine if you are really prioritizing your priorities
4. Identify time thieves and arrest them
5. Incorporate your priorities into your weekly routine.

My List of Priorities:

1._____

_____

2._____

_____

3._____

_____

4._____

_____

5._____

_____

3

Work-Life Balance, A Misnomer

Work-Life Balance or Life Balance

So, there is this concept the world has termed work-life balance, that has become a buzz word amongst employers and employees alike. As companies look for ways to enhance their benefits offerings, this is a term that is touted often. According to businessdictionary.com, work-life balance is defined as "A comfortable state of equilibrium, achieved between an employee's primary priorities of their employment position and their private lifestyle".

As I began to think about this, I challenged the actuality of the concept. To say that there needs to be a balance between your work and your life is to say that your work, job, or career, is actually separate and apart from your entire life. On the contrary, just like your family, ministry, hobbies, chores, etc., your work is **a part** of your life. Therefore, my belief is that we ought not to be striving for 'Work-Life Balance', but rather **Life Balance**. In fact, I will go as far as to say that there is no such thing as Work-Life Balance. Yep, I said it. You cannot balance work and life. This concept that many are striving for is impossible. I can hear many of you now saying, 'What do you mean?'

Well, work and life were NEVER meant to be balanced. Stay with me here. I'm saying that there is no such thing as Work-Life Balance because you cannot technically 'balance' two things when one is a part of the other. For instance, if work is A and life is B, you would have to take work, a portion of life, out of B in order to 'balance' the two. But, if you did this, you couldn't really balance the two because A would be missing a large part of its make-up. Let me explain this with a visual.

Here you will see a puzzle with nine pieces. Imagine that each puzzle piece represented one area of your life. Each piece is not <u>the</u> puzzle, rather each piece is <u>a part</u> of the puzzle. The entire object, with all nine pieces connected, is called a puzzle. Without all nine pieces being connected, it would not be a complete puzzle. Now, if *life* is the puzzle, and you remove *work*, one of the nine puzzle pieces, you no longer have a complete puzzle. *Work* is part of *Life's* puzzle. Therefore, you cannot accurately balance the complete puzzle of *life* with the one puzzle piece called *work*. Even if we analyzed this concept using measurements, work would still only be part of the whole or one-ninth. A part can never be balanced with or equal to the whole. Are you getting my point? Please reference the following diagrams.

Work   **Life**

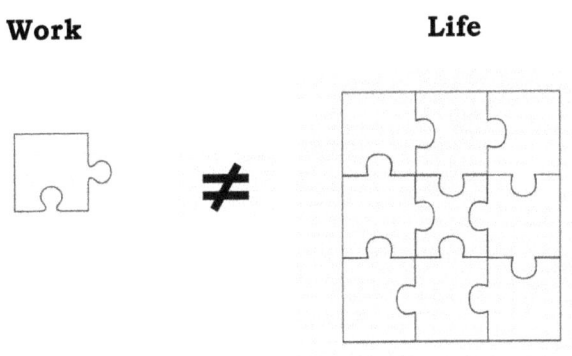

'Work–Life Balance'

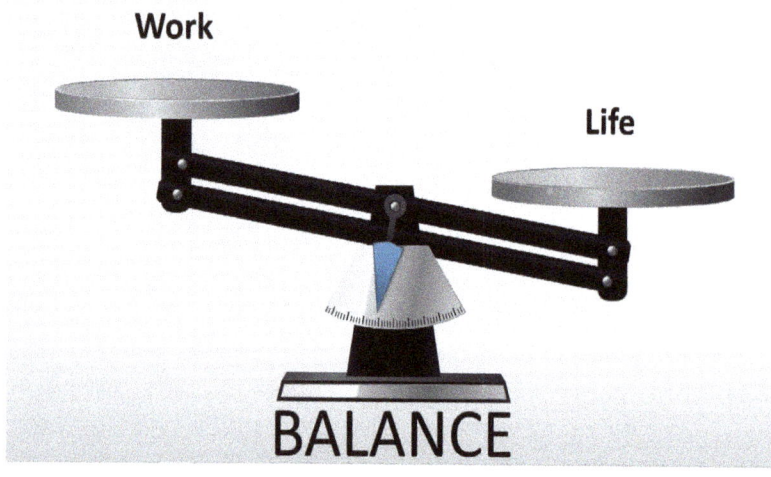

Life Balance

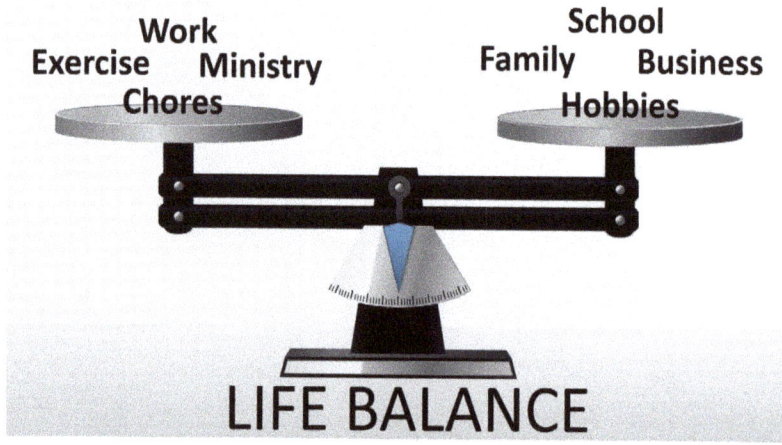

As you can see from the diagram of the scales, life will always be heavier than work. Life is actually the sum total of everything, including work. We have so many other competing interests in our everyday lives to focus solely on work. Is it the most important thing in our lives? Most Christians will tell you that God is the most important thing in their life. Yet, we don't hear people say that they need more 'God-Life Balance' do we? Of course not, because we live life in God, just like we do work in life. Every area of our lives requires balance, and every area of our lives is, well, a part of our life. We cannot extract work from our life's scale and then weigh it against our life. Life can never be equal to work. There will always be an imbalance between the two. So, let's dispel the misnomer of 'Work-Life Balance'.

But, how do we find balance? Here is what the Word says.

Commit your works to the LORD,
And your plans will be established.

~ Proverbs 16:3 (NASB)

*But don't begin until you **count the cost**. For who would begin construction of a building without first calculating the cost to see if there is enough money to finish it?*

~ Luke 14:18 (NLT)

*She considers a [new] field before she buys or accepts it **[expanding prudently and not courting neglect of her present duties by assuming other duties]**; with her savings [of time and strength] she plants fruitful vines in her vineyard.*
~ Proverbs 31:16 (AMP)

*Look carefully then how you walk, not as unwise but as wise, **making the best use of the time,** because the days are evil.*

~ Ephesians 5:15-16 (ESV)

*Teach us to number our days so that we may **truly live** and achieve wisdom.*

~ Ps 90:12 (VOICE)

These scriptures clearly tell us how to avoid being overloaded and overwhelmed. We are all juggling various responsibilities on a daily basis, whether intentionally or seemingly unintentionally. I say seemingly because this is a choice, and many times we are not thoroughly considering the potential impact of all of our commitments. We must count the cost and consider our present duties before assuming others. As you read this book, you may hear me say, more than once that, we all have 24 hours in each day that have already been given purpose. The question is, are we taking authority over our time, or are we letting time control us?

Let's go back to the example in one o'clock (chapter 1) about the food you put on your plate. Your life is like a plate. Each food group should have a place on your plate.

We all know about the recommended portion sizes and diversifying our food choices, but we don't always consider how this is also applicable to our lives. What are your recommended portion sizes for the various areas (food groups) of your life? These portions are not formulated by the U.S.D.A., but rather by the G.O.D.! Our God knows everything about everything, and He is willing to share it with you! Before you were formed in the womb, He knew you. Therefore, He is the only one that can give you the unique formula, the specific combination, the right portions that you need for proper life balance, according to His will.

Your Life in Equal Portions
(Not Prioritized and Unrealistic)

LIFE

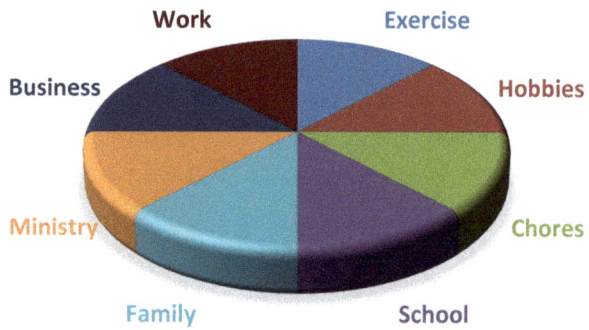

Your Life in Purposeful Portions
(Prioritized and Realistic)

LIFE

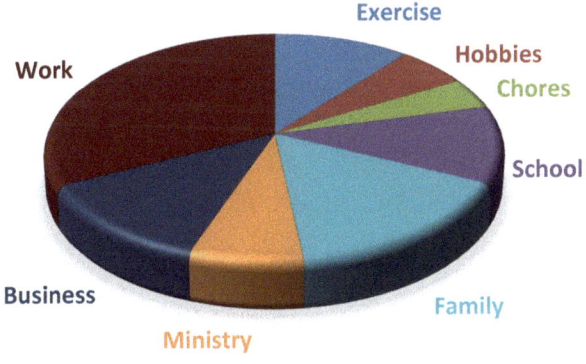

When we hear the term balance, we often correlate that with equal. Although this definition may be accurate in some instances, when it comes to life balance and time management, balance simply refers to the right proportions, as depicted in the pie diagram. Please note that this diagram is just an example to emphasize that not all parts of your life will require the same amount of time, nor should they have the same amount of weight, priority or importance. While it may not depict the exact portion sizes for your life, trust that God knows the size of your plate and how your pie should be sliced.

As His servant, you not only serve others, but you also serve yourself. Servants are also defined as helpers or waiters. A waiter waits or attends to the customer's needs.

As you serve, who are you really helping when you overload your plate? You are certainly not helping yourself. Are you actually waiting on God for instructions on how to meet your needs or provide the right balance for your life? Or, are you diving in head first and then screaming for a life raft?

We must remember that He is our helper, not just when we are drowning. In fact, He wants to help us before we even jump into the water. He has already laid out the perfect plan for our lives, but we have to allow Him to be our guide. Every step that we take either leads us closer to Him or, unfortunately, further away from Him. Although the way that we manage our time might seem trivial until something drastic occurs, see your days, your minutes, and your hours as steppingstones to your next destination. If you are allowing God to guide you, then you are on the right path. But if you are not leaning on Him for understanding about the way, you will walk yourself away from God's will for your life, delaying or denying the future that He planned for you.

Is it that serious? Yes, it is. God is a God of order, and since He has already laid out the plan for your life, He does not want you to deviate from it. This is why we must maximize every minute of our day. If we can manage our time, we can manage our life, purposefully! We MUST be purposeful about prioritizing our time to achieve the Life Balance that is required for the good success that He has promised.

Chapter Notes

4

Goal Setting, Getting, and Timing

STEP 1: **VISUALIZE IT** – SEE YOURSELF THERE

Is everything in your life going the way that you thought or envisioned? I think most would respond to this question with a resounding 'No'. How can we get our lives to line up with our faith confessions? Have you asked God? Are you meditating on the Word? Consider this... You create your reality! [SELAH]

We've all heard the saying, 'If you can see it, you can be it', but for too many of us, it is just that, a cute saying. If you don't see yourself successful, you won't be successful. If you don't see yourself overcoming, then you won't overcome. We have to see it before we SEE IT! So, focus on what you want to see and go for it. Notice that I didn't just say focus on what you see and leave it there. We have to focus on what we see and then do something about what we are seeing. Some of us are simply staring at the vision like we are hypnotized. Snap out of it now and go do the work. Faith without works is dead!

When visualizing, ensure that your goals are in alignment with the priorities that you identified previously. This is very important as we tend to focus on what needs to happen right now, like working, paying bills, etc. However, what is your ultimate goal? While we must take care of the immediate, we must also plan for the future. If we continue to put off God's desire for our life, we will live in discontentment, because as Psalms 37:4 states, "He gives us the desires of our heart". I believe this scripture to mean that not only does he give us the desire, as in placing it in our hearts, but he also gives us the desire by guiding us in what we need to do for it to manifest. He wants you to see it and so do I!

STEP 2: **TRANSCRIBE IT** – WRITE IT DOWN
FAILURE TO PLAN = PLANNED FAILURE

Where do you see yourself in the next year, 5 years, 10 years, etc.? Have you written down your goals? If not, let's change that today. Remember, if you fail to plan, you plan to fail.

What is your vision for your life? What is God's vision for your life? They should be the same. Remember, HE created YOU for HIS purpose! Habakkuk 4 admonishes us to write the vision and make it plain so that we can run with it. It literally answers the question of how our vision will be manifested. Once written, we can run with the written vision because it becomes the finish line that we focus on in the marathon of life.

What are your life goals?

1-year goals

___

___

___

___

5-year goals

___

___

___

___

10-year goals

___

___

___

___

STEP 3: **DESCRIBE IT –** BREAK IT DOWN

Now that we've identified your goals, how do you plan to accomplish them? Well, you must invest time into anything that you want to be successful at. Let's start by taking your vision and walking it backwards into small weekly steps. By creating a step-by-step guide, you are essentially scheduling your success. Execution of your time management plan or schedule allows you to guarantee progress.

So, what are your time management goals or what should they be? Compare the current schedule that you created in lesson 1 to the goals you listed in this lesson. Are your goals aligned with your schedule? Have you committed consistent time to your life goals? Are you doing things that don't align with your goals? Should you be doing more/less?

🛑 *Please make a copy of the next few pages so you can complete them for each set of 1-year, 5-year, and 10-year goals.*

Let's take a look at your _____ year goals.

Goal #_____

_____

_____

_____

_____

Ask yourself the following questions and note the answers below? (If you need some time to pray, research or think about this further, please take the time to do that before moving on.)

1. What can I do quarterly to meet this goal?

_____

_____

_____

2. What can I do monthly to meet this goal?

_____

_____

_____

_____

3. What can I do weekly to meet this goal?

_____

_____

_____

_____

Once you complete these questions for each goal, please go through a similar exercise for the remaining 1-year, 5-year, and 10-year goals. For the 5 and 10 year goals, you may not have a weekly task that you need to carry out at this time, but at a minimum you should have a quarterly task to accomplish.

STEP 4: **EXERCISE IT** - DO IT!

It's time to execute your plan. You have identified what is needed on a weekly basis to accomplish your goals. So, let's incorporate those tasks into your current schedule. In order to do this, you must first determine how much time is needed to accomplish this weekly task. Once you identify the time period, you will need to determine the ideal day(s) to carry this out consistently. Using your time management plan (created in the next chapter), please input the new tasks, ensuring that they can realistically be completed within the time allotted.

5
Time Management Essentials

TIME MANAGEMENT ESSENTIALS (TME)

Creating your Time Management Plan

TME #1 – GET ORGANIZED

Organization is key...

Gather your work calendar, your kids' school calendars, your family activities calendars, etc. You need to organize everything in one place, so make sure that you have a copy of ALL weekly and monthly schedules. We have a lot going on, but we can avoid being overwhelmed if we take the time to get organized. Only then can we thoroughly review everything that we have to consider as we become better time managers.

DRAFT YOUR CURRENT SCHEDULE

It is important for us to establish a baseline of your current situation so that we can accurately measure your progress during this program.

1. Start with a blank calendar and create your current weekly schedule. Please fill in the schedule type (ie. work, school, exercise, cleaning, etc.), start and end times for each of the schedules noted below.

a. Include the following on your schedule:
   i. Work schedule
   ii. Spouse's schedule (if applicable)
   iii. School schedule (if applicable)
   iv. Kid's school schedule (if applicable)
   v. Exercise schedule
   vi. Extracurricular schedule
   vii. Volunteer schedule
   viii. Other weekly/monthly schedules

b. Once you have completed your current schedule, verify its accuracy by taking a week to compare what you have written to what actually occurs during the week. Remember, to be honest during this comparison. If revisions need to be made, please do that before moving on to the next step.

⏲ TIME FOR ACTION!

When will you get organized?
Set a date and time!

TME #2 – PRIORITIZE

"Desires dictate our priorities, priorities shape our choices, and choices determine our actions."

— Dallin H. Oaks

Now that you have organized all of your calendars and schedules, it's time to prioritize. Review all of the information before you and determine what is MOST important. Once you have identified what is important, you will need to rank them in order of priority. This means that the obvious tasks like work and school (if you have kids) must be among your top priorities, while extracurricular activities will need to be worked around your core schedule. If your health is important to you, then (of course) exercise should be a top priority as well. You can't always do everything, but you should do the things that need to be done FIRST. Once you become more efficient with your time, you will be able to incorporate not just the things that need be done, but the things that you want to do as well. Take some time to meditate, inquire of the Lord and think about what your priorities are. Compare your Chapter 2 priorities and Chapter 4 goals. Write your revised list of priorities on the next page.

My Priorities

1. _____

_____

2. _____

_____

3. _____

_____

4. _____

_____

5. _____

_____

🕐 TIME FOR ACTION!

When will you prioritize your priorities?
Set a date and time!

TME #3- WRITE THE VISION

"When the vision is clear, the results will appear

— Terri Savelle Foy

Put pen to paper! Since you have already prioritized everything, you can start drafting your new time management plan. There are plenty tools available to help you to stay on task with your new time management plan. If you like old fashioned pen and paper, use a desk calendar or a daily planner to write everything down. If you are tech savvy, use your phone, tablet, or computer to document everything in one place, so that you can see what you have going on at any given moment and spot potential conflicts. Whatever method you choose, you must document, document, document. A thought unwritten remains a thought!

⏰ TIME FOR ACTION!

When will you write your vision?

Set a date and time!

TME #4 – COLLABORATE

"Alone we can do so little; together we can do so much"

— *Hellen Keller*

We are half-way through the TMEs and by this time you should have a draft time management plan to work with. If your calendar incorporates other people, co-workers, family members, etc., you need to discuss how you will accomplish those tasks with their help. Whether it's scheduling a meeting or ensuring that the kids are picked up on time, when your success depends on the participation of others collaboration is crucial.

⏰ TIME FOR ACTION!

Who will you collaborate with?
Set a date and time!

TME #5 - BE FLEXIBLE

"The measure of a person's strength is not his muscular power or strength, but it is his flexibility and adaptability."

— *Debasish Mridha*

Flexibility makes for a limber life! Know that interruptions will come, but they don't have to throw your schedule completely off. There are some things that you can plan for. For instance, plan a time cushion into your daily commute. If it takes 30 minutes to get to your destination, leave at least 15 minutes earlier. Keep some healthy snacks in the car in the event that you are delayed, to avoid that unhealthy fast food pit stop. Take a book or some work with you to an appointment and use your time wisely while you are in the waiting room. The point is -- allow some time for the unplanned, in your plan.

⏲ TIME FOR ACTION!

Create a plan to be more flexible.
Set a date and time!

TME #6 – EXECUTE THE PLAN

"There is value in careful planning and thoughtful preparation. However, until there is execution, no plan is flawed; no preparation inadequate. Execution spotlights all."
— Chip Bell

Now, a plan is just words on paper if it is not executed. The purpose of writing any plan is so that you can carry it out. If you are not used to structure in your life this will require some discipline, but hang in there. If you desire more control of your time, this is necessary. Your calendar or schedule is simply a time management plan. Now that you have created it, it's time to execute it. This means that you need to use it consistently. Don't be discouraged if it doesn't flow as planned on the first go-round. Just like anything else that you want to master, practice makes permanent.

⏰ TIME FOR ACTION!

When will you execute the plan?
Set a date and time!

TME #7 - BE WILLING TO CHANGE

True progress is measurable and change is inevitable!

"Those who cannot change their minds cannot change anything."

— George Bernard Shaw

It's okay to switch it up sometimes! Although change is inevitable, sometimes we just want to stick with what we've been doing. We become comfortable in what we know and distrust what we don't know. Meaningful change comes with discomfort, but when we focus on our goal, we can endure it.

While on Spring Break a several years ago, we took a road trip and visited 7 states. Our original plan was to visit 4 states. But, because our goal was to finish visiting all 50 states by the next summer, after reviewing our schedule, we made an adjustment to our plan, which put us closer to our goal.

How will you know that better is available if you don't do something different? You might be asking, 'what does this have to do with time management?' Well, in order to know if you can make a change to your schedule or time management plan, you must first have one. And, in order to determine whether your current plan is effective, you have to monitor it. You won't know how close you are to accomplishing your goal if it is not clearly defined, executed, measured and then modified, if necessary.

It is said that the only thing that is constant is change. It sounds like an oxymoron, but it's true. Just keep living and you will see that things change, including you! As the daily events of your life change, you will need to make adjustments to how you manage your time. A change in jobs or a change in your child's school will prompt a change in your daily routine. You may need to create a new time management plan. If you have taken advantage of the information provided in these TMEs, you've taken the right steps to become a better time manager. So, embrace change. You are prepared for the challenge!

⏲ TIME FOR ACTION!

Embrace Change!

It is inevitable.

Chapter Notes

RECAP

TIME MANAGEMENT ESSENTIALS (TMEs)

1. ORGANIZE
2. PRIORITIZE
3. WRITE THE VISION
4. COLLABORATE
5. BE FLEXIBLE
6. EXECUTE THE PLAN
7. BE WILLING TO CHANGE

Dr. Maunda Charles' Quotes for Time Management Success!

🕒 *Are you taking authority over your time, or are you letting time control you?*

🕒 *Time is costly. We can either spend it, waste it or invest it. You can tell which one you have done by the corresponding return that you receive.*

🕒 *Your time is not only precious, it's prophetic. So, use it purposefully!*

🕒 *You always have time for what you prioritize!*

🕒 *God has graced us to do everything that we are <u>supposed</u> to do. There is no grace for things that you should not be doing.*

🕒 *There is a purpose for every minute of your day and there is a time for every purpose!*

🕒 *Focus on those things that attract and attach you to your purpose, not those that detract or distract you from your purpose.*

🕒 *Procrastination not only delays your tasks, it potentially delays your purpose!*

🕒 *Your commitment to changing the way that you think about and manage your time will be the difference in whether you become the manager or the managed.*

6

My Time About Dr. Charles

Let me start by saying that I don't profess to be an expert on time management, I don't believe that everyone knows everything about everything, except God. However, I have experience, and Godly wisdom and insight. What I have shared in this book has been a proven methodology for time management success.

As I think back on my own time management journey, I recall having a very active childhood, from participating in sports, to extracurricular activities, to performing arts. However, I don't recall ever being consistently late for anything. That was, of course, when I was not responsible for managing my own time. If you are a parent reading this, your example is important, both in word and in deed.

In my household, many of the life lessons that I learned were not preached, but they were practiced. When I became a wife and mother, however, I recognized the value of both ways of training and teaching my family.

In the first year of master's program, I was a full-time student, a full-time employee, a part-time employee on the weekends, and an NCAA tennis player. I don't recall ever feeling stressed during this time, and this is the one and only semester that I was on the Dean's List (go figure). Looking back, what I realized is that I had developed a strategy for effectively managing my time.

Earlier in this book, I mentioned that I definitely needed to master time management once we had children, for my own sanity. This is still true today. As of the time of me writing the second edition of Manage Your Time, Manage Your Life...Purposefully, we now have three adult children and two in high school. The need for time management has not diminished.

While we are no longer responsible for being the taxi drivers for all five of our children, we still have two that have very involved schedules. In addition to that, our personal schedules have become even more complex as our responsibilities in business and ministry have increased. If you are seeking to fulfill purpose and accomplish all that you are supposed to in this life, mastering time management will always be essential. How you execute the plan will change, but the need for a plan will not.

Our God is the God of order and so are His plans for us. We will not always know or see how He is orchestrating our paths, but we should definitely be cognizant of the fact that there is a path, and it consists of us committing each and every day to Him. Every step we take that is contrary to path that He has already laid out, will lead us down a road that is further away from our purpose. Who really wants to waste time? I'm all about efficiency. I don't have time to waste, and I don't want to work harder when I can work smarter. If you are reading this book, I know that you feel the same way. So, make every day count. Let's manage our time, so we can manage our lives, purposefully!

7

Family Time

Purposeful Time Management & My Family

The scripture is clear when it states that we must first be able to manage our homes before attempting to manage any outside entity. If I was not utilizing my own product or service, I would not expect you to believe in it, much less purchase it. My family is my first ministry. So, on the next few pages, I wanted to leave you with their perspectives on purposeful time management and how it has and continues to help them. I hope this glimpse of their inside view is helpful.

Over the past 40 years, the size of the American family has seen steady decreases from 3.13 to 2.53 persons per household in 2018. Although 0.60 doesn't seem like a huge difference, with a seven-person household, our family more than doubles the national average. As a result, my wife and I are constantly entertained with looks of bewilderment when people discover that we have 5 children. "You have how many children?" and "how do you do it?", are just a few of the many questions we get, particularly when we meet people for the first time. It is almost like we have some deep ancient secret or potion that allows us to maintain our youthful vigor while managing a household of nonstop enthusiasm.

Originating from the tranquil shores of the laid-back Caribbean, it is nothing short of a miracle that we have managed the hustle and bustle of modern-day American life. With children at every school level, extracurricular activities, ministry obligations, and sports activities, there is 'seemingly' no time. Nevertheless, we have found a mechanism to not just maintain our sanity but position each family member with the opportunity to pursue their dreams and aspirations.

No matter who you are, where you are from, or your economic status, we all are unified in that we all have 24-hours in each day. As shocking of a revelation that may be to many, we don't get an extra 2-hours because we have a larger family than most. How you manage those 24-hours will determine if you continue feeling devoid of enough time to arrive on time to your activities, get a sufficient amount of sleep or stopped feeling seemingly rushed for everything. Managing time is not just managing your schedule; it is managing your life.

One of the biggest adjustments living in the metropolitan Washington DC area has been the consistency of traffic, and the ever-present temptation to rush through every activity due to the perceived or realized lack of time. This culture of constant busyness has no shortage of time stealers; whether they are legitimate activities such as commuting across the county to a school activity or navigating the beltway to grocery shop, it just doesn't seem like there is ever enough time.

Having worked in the land development field for almost twenty years, it can be quite a challenge to maintain a consistent life balance while advancing professionally. For too many of my colleagues, they have become almost like strangers to their families while growing professionally. As easy as it is to see this in others, this unbalanced lifestyle has not always been easily recognized when evaluating myself.

As a sports enthusiast and basketball player most of my life, I knew I had arrived at a tipping point when I couldn't find a few minutes within my day to even make a couple layups much less play a few games. It seemed like no matter how hard I tried, there was some other competing activity crouching at my door. What made it more complex is that these 'perceived' time conflicts were not unethical or harmful activities to my spiritual or physical well-being, they were legitimate and necessary functions like school activities for the kids, work, errands, etc.; 24-hours was seemingly just not enough as I continued to reduce my sleep time to try and compensate for the seemingly growing lack of time.

However, recognizing that I was growing somewhat disgruntled, my wife decided to purchase a basketball rim that I could use at home for myself and the kids, but more importantly, developed a strategic plan that would allow me to complete my weekly obligations while providing a window of time for active relaxation, shooting basketball. What I lacked was not time, but a personalized plan for my time so I could accomplish my goals and desires.

To some, this scenario may seem farfetched and even a little trivial, however, her discernment and ability to help me solve this 21st Century dilemma for my specific situation was timely and provided a greater appreciation for the importance of time management.

Looking back on this and many other experiences where I have directly benefited from her ability to discern the time, I am left wondering how this evolution of time appreciation grew within an individual from a laid-back Caribbean culture of "we will get to it when we get to it". What I see is an individual who thoroughly understands that time is not only money, but time is our most precious resource; time is synonymous with life. Therefore, if you find yourself, like so many of us today, where there are seemingly not enough hours in a day to meet your goals, complete your tasks, bring order to your life, let this book serve as a reminder that there is a way of escape for you, and time management provides a door for you to get there.

Soneil Charles
Husband (2019)

Purposeful time management has been critical for me in all aspects of my life. Whether it is managing people, projects, or priorities, it is essential in allowing me to maximize my daily potential without being overwhelmed or unproductive. I find that the times when I don't have a plan for my time, I am more susceptible to being distracted and accomplish much less in my day than when I do. As a husband, father, son, friend, ministry leader and corporate professional, there are many things clamoring for my time during my wake hours. Therefore, managing my time purposefully is not an occasional hobby, it has become a staple for my personal wellbeing and meaningful contributions to the lives of others. Simply put it is ABSOLUTE NECESSITY! Although I have a lot more room for growth, I see how I have progressed over the past few years of intentionally working on being purposeful with my time and I strongly recommend you personally committing to the principles outlined in this book. Not only will you see the benefits of these principles yourself, but those around you will reap the benefits of your purposeful investment in your most precious resource, time!

Soneil Charles
Husband (2025)

Purposeful time management has helped me realize that the saying "Time is of the Essence" is truly an accurate statement. My mom has always been big on creating schedules for everything. As much as I used to dislike the idea of writing everything down, I've realized that planning helps me keep track of so much more than events/activities I already know about.

Planning and creating schedules allows me to review my week and see where I have openings for any last minute activities that might arise. It is so important to create a schedule because I can't force my brain to remember every single thing I have to do. I have been able to maximize my time by using purposeful time management so that I can accomplish my priorities and also make time for things I want to do as well.

It's important to make the most of your time here on earth so that we can maximize the gifts that God has given us. We have so much to give and so much to offer. But, if we don't use our time wisely, how will we be able to accomplish everything we have set in our hearts to do? Everyone has the same 24 hours. It's what you do in those 24 hours that counts.

Sonayah Charles, 19
Daughter (2019)

Time management has helped me a lot because I now help other people manage their time and their daily life from the tools I've learned. My calendar has become one of my greatest assets in life and really helps me to stay organized and on top of my tasks. I manage a lot of different ministries, groups and people, so proper time management is key to ensuring that I can actually be effective and productive in all of those things.

With a lot of personal endeavors myself, sometimes it can seem like I have an overwhelming amount of things to do. But with the proper measures in place, I'm able to get things done. Time is one of the greatest currencies we have in life, so I'm learning more and more to value it. Everything in our lives requires time, so why not make the most of it?

Sonayah Charles, 25
Daughter (2025)

Purposeful time management, a.k.a. my mom, helps me to stay focused and stop procrastinating. With her help, I manage my schedules. She also helps manage my art business, etc. Purposeful time management has helped me to keep track of what I need to do and helped me to make sure I get everything done in a select time, so that I don't forget to do it later.

Jael Charles, 16
Daughter (2019)

Time management has been a game-changer in my role as a creative, allowing me to balance the demands of creating, editing, and publishing content while meeting deadlines. By allocating specific time blocks for brainstorming ideas, scripting, filming, and editing, I ensure that each project gets the attention it needs without feeling rushed. Planning ahead also helps me stay consistent with posting schedules and overall balance it with my work-life, creative-life and social-life. With strong time management skills, I can produce high-quality content regularly, avoid burnout, and continue to engage my audience effectively. Time management also helps me stay creative and artistic by providing structure without stifling spontaneity. By setting aside dedicated blocks of time for brainstorming, experimentation, and refining ideas, I give myself the space to explore new concepts while staying on track with deadlines. This balance between planning and flexibility allows me to avoid feeling overwhelmed and gives me the freedom to approach each project with fresh energy. With a clear schedule, I can also prioritize breaks and downtime, which are essential for recharging my creativity and maintaining inspiration over time.

Jael Charles, 22
Daughter (2025)

Time management has impacted me because it has made me a more organized person overall and also has helped me to not waste time in my daily life. Time management is important because it helps you achieve your goals by knowing what you want to do, when you need to do it by, and how much time you need to be able to complete the task before starting it. Since I'm still in school, I have to manage my time outside of school and inside of school in order to receive the best grades possible. I have to plan out my days and organize my assignments in order to get the results I want to see on my report card. Time management is a big help when you are trying to be successful in or at anything in life.

Nailah Charles, 15
Daughter (2019)

Time management has helped to improve my quality of life. I say this because once I learned the skill of time management, every area in my life became more organized. It became so organized that I realize I actually have more time in the day than I thought I did, which leaves me more time to get more things done. I use time management on a daily basis whether it's in my personal life, at work or serving in ministry; time management applies to all areas of life.

Nailah Charles, 20
Daughter (2025)

Having a schedule helps me because I can manage how much time I need for the things I do. Also, it helps me to not go over the time that is set to stop what I am doing. When I use a schedule, I can make sure that I get everything done that I need to do. Schedules keep me on track for what I need to do.

Adanya Charles, 11
Daughter (2019)

As a junior in high school, I have been told multiple times that this is my most important year of high school; a heavier workload, college applications, and extracurriculars. For someone who doesn't have good time management skills, this year could definitely become stressful. I have found a way to manage this year through time management, organization, and figuring out what works well for me. I have found how to get what I need to do done, while still having free time. Time management is the key to that life balance.

Adanya Charles, 16
Daughter (2025)

Having a schedule helps me because I can check if I have to do something or if I skipped something. Also, I can see if I am late to do something. Plus, it helps me to remember things I need to do. Sometimes I want to do other things, but when I look at the schedule it helps me to stay focused.

Caleb Charles, 9
Son (2019)

Time management has helped me in ways like being able to complete more things in one day. Having a plan makes it easier to complete your tasks for the day. It also helps you be more consistent with your tasks. When you have a plan for every day, it helps build repetition. Doing all this will make your days easier if you just stay consistent with it.

Caleb Charles, 15
Son (2025)

I hope you enjoyed hearing from my family. I would love to hear how this book has impacted you and your family. Please feel free to share your experience by emailing me. Lastly, have you discovered your purpose in life? Well, I have one final word to share with you on the next page.

DISCOVERING YOUR PURPOSE
(Time for a New Beginning)

Throughout this book, we have been discussing the importance of identifying your purpose and priorities in the process of time management. As with any product that you purchase, in order to determine its intended purpose or address any malfunction in the product, we must go back to the manufacturer or the instruction manual for clarity or corrective measures. We want the product to function as intended because we paid for it, with the expectation that it would work properly.

In the same way, the only way to discover our purpose, and whether we are actually fulfilling it, is to ask our manufacturer, our creator, God. However, the ability to ask Him is contingent upon our relationship with Him. Just like we had to purchase the product in order to inquire or communicate with the manufacturer, there was a sacrificial purchase made over 2000 years ago, that allows us to have relationship with God. He longs for a relationship with you. Allow the Creator to define your purpose. He is calling. Will you answer? Say this prayer out loud.

I confess with my mouth, the Lord Jesus, and believe in my heart that God has raised him from the dead, therefore I am saved. With my heart I believe unto righteousness; and with my mouth confession is made unto salvation.

If you prayed this prayer sincerely, let me be the first to welcome you to the family of God! All of heaven is rejoicing about your decision for Christ and I am too! The next step in your kingdom development is to connect with a Bible-believing, Bible-teaching ministry, where you can grow in the Word. If you need assistance with this, please feel free to email me at the address below for a recommendation on a ministry in your area, or consider Faith City Central.

timemanager@purposefultime.com

@drmikefreeman

@FaithCityCentral

A Wife, Mother of five children, Minister, Teacher, Author, Entreprenuer, Chief Administrative Officer of several family businesses and Chief Family Officer of the Charles household, Dr. Maunda Charles understands the necessity for Life Balance. She has an MBA in Business Administration and a Doctorate in Christian Leadership and Entrepreneurship. Dr. Charles is a former Survey Statistician, Program Analyst and Administrative Officer for the U.S. federal government. She is currently the Executive Officer and Director of Quality Assurance at Faith City Central, as well as the Operations Manager for The Fellowship. Dr. Charles is a master of PURPOSEFUL TIME MANAGEMENT. She believes that "identifying purpose and priority is key to achieving Life Balance".

www.purposefultime.com

www.ingramcontent.com/pod-product-compliance
Lightning Source LLC
LaVergne TN
LVHW051039070526
838201LV00066B/4865